Time Management Skills for Kids (Over 12)

Time Management Workbook for Kids to Be Productive and Live a Purposeful Life

By

C. Franklin
TSB Publications

About the Author

C. Franklin has been a well-known name in the domain of Kids E-books related to multiple genres. He specializes in coming up with books for kids based on skills that they need to learn in order to become productive in life. The core idea behind his writing style is to introduce activity-based books having a practical nature so that kids may understand and practice the given concepts for a better understanding.

Table of Contents

Introduction

Learning to organize their own time is among the most crucial life skills that kids pick up during their schooling. Numerous kids struggle to find enough time to do their assignments or for studying which may turn them into angry, irritated, and overwhelmed souls. Nonetheless, if they manage their time wisely, they may be able to focus on all aspects of their academic life and study effectively.

Kids over 12 are just about to enter their teenage years in some time and it is extremely important to make them realize the importance of time management in their lives. The idea is to make them more efficient from a younger age so they may know how to get rid of issues like procrastination and mismanagement of daily activities.

Kids can focus more closely on a task when you set a time frame. Following the schedule will increase your chances of completing the task as compared to starting without a plan. Think about finishing your projects or finishing your schoolwork timely. If you don't set aside some time to concentrate on things, you'll probably forget to complete them. However, if you keep a decent schedule, you can devote adequate time to each assignment to achieve your goals.

If you use your time wisely, you can complete your assignments on time. You also get a feeling of confidence and self-reliance in your abilities as a result of this. Comparable feelings might result from crossing off a long list of tasks, which can serve as motivation to do better at time management. Even outside of the classroom, being organized can be useful. The book *Time Management Skills for Kids* is a comprehensive collection of all the advice and methods to improve your time managerial skills. You will be not be able to accomplish much if you don't stick to a regular timetable, regardless of how diligent you are or whether you find the time for enjoyable things or not. Learning the fundamentals of effective time planning and task organization is not at all that difficult.

The goal is to live a disciplined life and to avoid wasting time on activities that won't benefit you in the long-term, therefore, you must pay full attention to time management if you want to progress successfully and become more productive. Learning about such methods will make your lifestyle more disciplined, organized and timelier. Even if procrastinating would attempt to prevent you from achieving your goals, you will feel more motivated to say no to it while being time managed.

You won't get any closer to your true objectives if you don't respect time in your normal activities. Therefore, it is advised that you must become familiar with the best and effective methods to utilize your limited time as efficiently as possible. In regards to learning the most efficient time management strategies, this very eBook you are going to read is a fantastic piece of literature. You have come to the perfect platform, and carefully reading the material here, will assist you in becoming a successful individual in your upcoming life. Put an end to your procrastinating now and begin implementing the strategies that you will discover in the book's upcoming chapters.

Chapter 1: What is Time Management?

The idea of trying to cram everything you've got and desire to do it in the few hours after schooling overwhelms most of you. There is a lot to accomplish between homework, hobbies, and just having free time to play and enjoy. However, even though most children don't have the intellectual capabilities to freely arrange their schedules until junior high, you may start by learning how to prioritize and arrange your time instantaneously.

1.1 Value of Time Management in Life

The technique of scheduling your free time and limiting the number of hours you devote to particular projects in order to function more effectively is known as time management. Some people organize their lives better than others, but anyone can acquire habits that will help them to handle their time more effectively.

Your Performance Will Improve

You will better analyze what you need to do and how long will each activity take when you manage to schedule time for your workday for all of your critical duties. If you have a timetable to stick to, you'll probably discover that you spend fewer hours debating what else to work on or putting off crucial tasks and even delaying them. You may concentrate on only the prioritized activities at hand and avoid time-wasting diversions by using time effectively.

Improves your Productivity

If you're not scrambling to finish a project by a certain date, you may devote more time and consideration to it. You may prioritize your work by managing time, ensuring that you have allocated adequate time to finish each assignment. If you're not in a hurry to do anything before a rapidly approaching date, your work level improves.

You Follow a Schedule

Giving each item on your checklist, a dedicated time slot, can help you to manage your time effectively. Many teens and adults utilize time effectively to give themselves more time to finish a project or to accomplish it before the deadline to give themselves some room to maneuver, in case some problems emerge. You'll be able to meet the deadlines if you plan the time required to accomplish your tasks.

You Becomes Less Stressed

If you have a long list of chores to complete both for your study and your leisure time or extra-curricular activities, it's simple to feel nervous. In order to know precisely what has to be done and the amount of time you have to finish it, you may prioritize your to-do lists and reserve the time required for the most critical chores with the aid of proper time management. Setting priorities for your projects and allowing yourself sufficient time to complete them will make you feel less stressed.

Enhanced Career Possibilities

Your capacity to manage your time effectively will make you a much more dependable worker in future who consistently turns in the high-caliber work on time. This will increase your value as a co-worker too and will enhance your professional reputation once you enter the professional life, both of which can result in new career-expanding options.

Increases Your Confidence
You'll get a sense of satisfaction and trust in your skills when you successfully control your time and meet your goals. Completing your everyday to-do list regularly can motivate people to enhance their time managerial skills and avail new opportunities.

1.2 Reasons Why Time Management is Vital for Kids

Children can prepare themselves for success by learning time management as a survival tool. For children to succeed in their schooling and other aspects of their life, they must study at a young age. Being able to organize one's time effectively as a child might help him to concentrate on his objectives and complete work without feeling overburdened.

Children may find it difficult to organize their time, but teaching them these lifelong skills at a young age is advantageous. When finishing coursework, concentrating on these stages is a fantastic place to start since other things will probably come along as you go. When children learn to control and manage their time, they will feel less burdened, which will increase their sense of accomplishment and self-assurance as they continue to accomplish in all spheres of their lives.

The ability to control their time helps kids to prioritize their work and to determine how much time each task will take. It aids in timely completion of tasks and teaches students how to set and follow a timetable. The capacity to effectively execute step-by-step instructions, a proper sense of obligation to finish homework and multitasking are skills that kids frequently need to practice.

Kids with good time-management abilities at home are more likely to finish their tasks or domestic obligations on schedule and to prepare for and leave the house on time every morning. Children with poor skills in time management might have a history of skipping school, putting off doing their schoolwork, rushing through it, and staying awake late to finish the projects. Academic achievement is greatly influenced by time management skills, which ranges from being aware of the importance of preparations to have a solid understanding of how long the projects can take to being able to prioritize the tasks. Continue reading for some typical instances of how schedule affects students' reading, composition, and math skills.

Encourage Them to Become Time-Conscious
It's critical to keep in mind that time is short. Evaluate all the chores that need to be finished, then divide things into manageable portions by prioritizing and scheduling. Have a conversation with your kid to assist them in understanding what is essential and crucial so that they can know from where to start. To demonstrate to your child that how much time is allowed for various categories like curricular,

extracurricular activities, family activities, etc., describe the concept of splitting each things in parts to them.

Establish a Timetable and a Routine

A timetable will help your child to stay on track whether they are studying as a hostelite or a day-scholar. You should also schedule additional classes like exercise or painting besides lunch and break. Include any additional after-school events or occasions that they ought to be informed of. Your youngster will benefit from knowing what and how to anticipate and how to get ready for their day.

Make the timetable with your child once you know what to prioritize. Make the procedure enjoyable! Encouraging kids to work on a graphical board with graphics, putting the time intervals on a calendar and color-coding it, putting stickers, or embellishing it with artwork are all effective ways to accomplish this.

Monitor Results and Consider the Time Spent

Follow your child's progress as they finish assignments to determine whether there are any opportunities for improvement or successes to be proud of. Collectively, you may think back on what transpired during that period to determine if they need to re-evaluate their time allocation in the upcoming time and learn how to make a strategy accordingly. Your youngster will be motivated to keep setting aside some time and organizing for future goals if they see how their well-spent effort resulted in success.

Honor Even Modest Accomplishments

Recognizing minor victories is one of the best ways to get kids to control their time. It's a huge accomplishment to finish assignments and stay close to the primary objective! Appreciate your child's accomplishments by praising them and pushing them to keep improving while regulating their playtime. They will be more motivated to carry out these initiatives in the future if they can see that their efforts have paid off.

1.3 Common Time Management Mistakes

For the majority of children, schooling is the first place where they have more unrestricted liberty to spend their time as they like. However, the importance of time management becomes even higher when kids come to age around 12 years and are ready to hit teenage years soon. Regrettably, very few of us develop time management abilities in school. As a result, when given the opportunity to do as we like, we often alternate between times of laziness and panicked races to do a term's amount of reading in one night. Here, I will discuss the worst time management mistakes that kids make in schools and colleges.

1. They Lack a Strategy

Most students don't have a strategy further than a list of tasks and due dates for completion. Many pupils give this very little thought. Existing in such a way simply invites tragedy such as:

- *You'll find three or more major tasks due the next day.*
- *You didn't have enough time to ask your tutor a question.*
- *You have all sorts of other issues.*

When the day begins, you must always understand what you're going to do. Preferably, you ought to have a clear idea of your schedule for the next week or two.

2. Before Exams, they Work Long Hours

Research repeatedly demonstrates that doing an all-nighter before such a test or exam is more harmful than useless. You will find it hard to recall what you tried to memorize, and your mind won't function well the next day anyway. It might require some planning over the entire duration of a semester and may take up more of your energy, yet it won't guarantee you to retain the material on test day and, most likely, even years later. In other words, getting sufficient sleep always wins over staying up late.

3. Mess in Their Study Region

What is its relationship to managing time? You only waste time in hunting for what you require when studying in a disorganized setting, wherein, you don't understand where everything is located. The things in your line of vision can quickly divert your attention. Many things around you divert your focus, making you reluctant to begin learning. To guarantee optimal concentration, you must preferably only have the present subject of your study right in front of you.

4. They are Unaware of When they are Most Effective

Each individual has distinct times of the day when they are most and least productive. Additionally, various periods of the day might be more or less effective for certain tasks. You could only figure out what these time spans are for you via trial and error. Try re-arranging your timetable; you might discover, for instance, that by scheduling your studying time before midday, you can do double a lot in the same number of hours as when you attempt this job in the afternoon.

5. There is No Priority Setting

We're not simply talking about prioritizing your education above your social life. Twenty per cent of the work yields 80 per cent of the outcomes, if done efficiently. If you do not have sufficient time to complete your whole to-do list, focus your energy on what is most crucial rather than attempting to accomplish everything. Avoiding these mistakes will make your time in school and college considerably less difficult and pleasurable.

Use the following time tracker to track your time for three days and make more such trackers, to manage your time well.

Name: _____   **Date:** _____

Time Tracker

Use this worksheet to track how much time you spend on each task in a day. Observe it for some days.
You can add anyother activity you do in the blank spaces given below.

Tasks	Day 1	Day 2	Day 3
Brushing and taking shower			
Taking breakfast			
Getting things ready for school			
Time spent with friends			
Playing and other fun activities			
Time spent watching TV			
Study, home work			
Doing chores around house			
Eating dinner			
Preparing the bed, and other prior sleep activities			

Chapter 2: Science of Setting Goals & Procrastination

Setting goals can be termed as one of the most effective approaches to boosting children's performance and motivation. Parents must be aware of some traps and misconceptions when assisting their children with setting one. Children require several useful specific skills, including the capacity to recognize, monitor, and achieve objectives, to be self-assured and to find success. However, teaching children how to create goals frequently takes a backseat in educating them on how and where to execute other activities. Help children develop this ability early rather than allowing them "find their way" when laying out short- and long-term objectives. Your dedication will help them by giving them a better feeling of direction and control.

2.1 Why is Goal Setting Important for Kids?

It might be challenging for some children to understand the ultimate goal as they grow up, study and attend school. To put it in another way, some children find it challenging to understand that the big picture is bigger than their last year's marks or the next week's test. It takes time to instill a more forward-thinking perspective in children; initially, they must absorb and comprehend that they won't always remain school children and won't be always spoon-fed to do something.

On the other hand, they must be aware that when they are grownups, they will be forced to make their own decisions and be given the liberty of doing so. When that realization sinks in, it's time to make conclusions about how their calculus class will help them to succeed as adults. What else should they now be studying in school in order to accomplish their goals? Setting objectives is crucial for children since it gives them a feeling of direction for their activities.

Having relevant and reasonable goals also has a lot of additional advantages. In addition to a host of many other positive effects, they aid with judgement, boost self-esteem and autonomy and teach persistence. Kids will have the drive to act, execute, and accomplish if they have a long-term goal of becoming expert coders, for instance. Crucially, students now understand that in order to get anywhere, they must first create smaller goals.

Attending college is one of those minor ambitions which calls for better grades, which is motivated by finishing work, and is fueled by studying objectively, which in turn is supported by school activities, and so on. Without any objective, schoolwork is only completed since a teacher says so, and extra-curricular activities aren't even taken into consideration since, in their eyes, playing games in their free time is a greater use of their schedule.

Make goals for yourself, your kids and then discuss them with your child or, your pupils, if you're teaching, since this is one of the finest ways to teach the idea of making objectives. You could be preparing to run a 5K, for example. If so, put your big goal—"Complete a 5K Race"—on the front of a sheet of paper, and then list all the steps you'll take to get there. These might include setting a weekly mileage goal, increasing the number of healthy foods you consume or getting a good pair of running shoes.

Request your child to assist you in achieving your own goals by walking them through those. Youngsters like lending a hand to their adult mentors. You'll not only receive a devoted supporter, but you'll also show your kid the fun and benefits of making goals.

Invite your child to attempt goal-setting once your target is underway or finished. Here are some suggestions for helping primary school kids make realistic learning objectives.

You can establish quantifiable, realistic learning goals with your kid (or student). However, it may take longer than anticipated to achieve the goals because life happens. Work alongside your child to rewrite the original solution if you encounter hurdles. Maybe the goal must be divided into smaller components because it was too complicated. Perhaps it isn't as important as just another objective that requires more immediate attention. Generally, keep an upbeat and motivating attitude. These are wise teachings for life.

Instructing a child how and where to modify their goals — while still maintaining them — encourages imagination and pragmatism. Thanks to this practice, you are now allowed to engage in intellectual discussions regarding goals. When they begin to get the feel of it, youngsters may feel really wise whenever it comes to setting objectives.

2.2 How Kids Can Set Goals?

Do you have questions about how youngsters can create goals and the advantages of their development? You don't need to panic any longer because you're about to learn the best suggestions for assisting your kids in setting realistic goals in life. Kids may set objectives that are so lofty or outside of their comfort zone that achieving them becomes almost difficult. Encourage your children to select achievable goals. Make sure your youngster comes up with the objective no matter what it is. The aim must mean something to your kid if you want them to stick with it.

Everyone loves to feel accomplished after completing a task. That makes sense. Sometimes children try to succeed by remaining entirely within their comfort bubble. Setting goals teaches us to strive, which is wonderful. We try to be innovative. Even if we don't complete a task in the allotted time, we could come close to it. Tryouts are worthwhile. Children must be taught to attempt. Encourage them to select objectives that are not only beyond reach, but also the reachable ones. By doing this, kids develop the ability to push themselves to take on new challenges rather than staying in their comfort bubble.

Try the following worksheet to make your small goal effective and approachable.

Name: _____   Date: _____

My Goal

My goal is ......

[ ]

To fill my goal, I will ......

[ ]

Different steps I will take to accomplish my goal......

[ ]

My Goal is important to me, because.......

[ ]

Create A Bucket List

Do you have kids? Encourage them to develop a physical or digital bucket list for their family or themselves. They can use their technological expertise and inventiveness in this situation. They can assist the family to track things online and share their checklists with them. This is a fantastic approach to involving local children in community activity and fostering relationships.

A bucket list often includes things a person hopes to achieve, encounter, or accomplish over their lifespan. You can make an annual bucket list to help your kids learn about the main objective while having fun. If the entire family participates, it becomes more enjoyable. What you should do is:

Get your family members, get some crayons and a sheet of chart paper, and begin brainstorming. Talk about your family's aspirations for the upcoming year regarding activities, adventures, and accomplishments.

Place the document in a prominent location where everybody may view it after brainstorming is complete. Your families will have a great time crossing things off the list as they are completed throughout the year.

You might discuss if you intend to achieve each of these objectives or whether your family's objectives have altered as the year progresses and you discover that there are still a few things left to do. How do you go about achieving them if you still would like to? What procedures must you adhere to?

According to research, kids can learn well through encounters compared to play. Your child will learn a great deal about goal-setting and tracking progress, and your whole family or community will enjoy doing it together.

You can review all that your household or neighborhood has achieved this year when it comes to an end. You may even start a new family/community custom by making the creation of a yearly wish list of shot-on-target events!

Establish A Vision Board

Your child will quickly picture their goals with a sketch pad. With this useful art and craft project, your kid will also enjoy himself. What you should do is:

Ask your kids to clip out images that symbolize their aspirations from some old magazines. You can download images from the internet if your kid is looking for a certain image that they are unable to locate in magazines.

The drawings will then be adhered to on a sheet of poster board by your kid. Additionally, they can be embellished with paint, sparkles, feathers, etc. When it's done, put the vision board in your kid's bedroom so they may see it often and be informed of their goals. Creating the vision board encourages your kid to consider their objectives and is a potent reminder of all that they want to accomplish.

Consider the vision board concept again and again. Discuss with your child the various images and how they intend to realize their varied aspirations. Help your child to divide a large objective into manageable chunks. Write down a few quick actions they can take right now to cut short their lengthy objectives.

Your youngster will acquire the skills of goal-setting, critical thinking, and planning. Additionally, he will also learn that his actions now and, in the future, are important and can have a beneficial influence. You can use the following vision board as an example and make your short and long term goals in it.

My vision board plans

Health Goals

Study Goals

Behavior Goals

Personal Grooming
Goals

Notes to stay stick with goals.

Create a Fortune Wheel

Author and expert on personal development, Dennis Whitley developed the concept for the wheel of fortune. What you should do is:

Assist your kid in drawing a wheel using sections. Your kid will list significant life areas in each part, such as home, friendships, schools, sports, etc.

Then, your kid will decide which area they want to concentrate on first. They will list every objective that they wish to complete under this area in a specific amount of time. For instance, if "Tennis" is the subject, your child can indicate that they want to practice at least three times per week, work on their backhand, and understand how to serve.

After that, discuss with your child the actions they will undertake to realize these objectives and any potential roadblocks. What will they accomplish to overcome these challenges if they do run across them?

The wheels can be colored and embellished any way in which your kid pleases; after that, hang them prominently.

Perform something to **CELEBRATE** after your child completes a section of the wheel, then continue the process for the next part. Your kid will gradually improve in many areas of their life while also learning how to set and accomplish objectives.

With the help of your kids, make a spin wheel to choose what activity should they do first by spinning the wheel. For this wheel, after writing the activities, ask your kid to move the finger around the wheel to choose what must be the next.

2.3 Relationship Between Goal Setting & Time Management

Can you describe the connection between goal-setting and time management? It's an easy query. The solution is easy to discern but putting it into words is challenging.

Firstly, without objectives, long-term planning is impossible. For instance, it occurs if you do nothing. You shouldn't view it; it is a waste of your time. You lack objectives. However, you'll consider the time passed if you make a goal. How can you get there on time? Or, when you have several objectives, you'll consider how to cut down on time required to achieve each one.

The second is that you have excellent time management abilities. It is challenging to develop these abilities if you don't have a purpose. Although it is not obvious, it is simple to comprehend. You lack the drive to act if you do not have a goal. It is challenging to accomplish anything, especially developing skills in time management, if you lack the motivation.

Third, since it is difficult to establish a deadline for a reason, it is difficult to accomplish the main goal without time management. In most cases, it would be beneficial if you could advance your objective. You set a modest time frame, but you are highly motivated. Self-discipline then comes to your aid. You become more effective because you acquire new skills, forgo lesser opportunities, and are given more time to accomplish your task.

2.4 Why Procrastination Can Affect Your Goals?

Despite what the majority claims, procrastination rarely involves getting inefficient. In reality, we often work furiously for extended periods right before our obligations when we delay. Laziness is the antithesis of working hard. Hence, it can't be why we put in all the effort. What is the main reason that causes us to put things off, and more importantly, what could we do to stop it?

Coping with a kid who procrastinates can be difficult and irritating for parents. Daily routines can be challenging enough to manage; therefore, everybody suffers when a kid neglects his duties. However, there are explanations for your child's delay, and you may be surprised. Occasionally, kids put off doing their chores, completing their schoolwork, or handling other duties since they don't want to. However, there are other situations when children put things off.

What's Causing Your Child to Put Things Off?
They don't know what's required of them: Kids may put off doing their chores, schoolwork, or other responsibilities since they do not even know what they are required to do. When a kid is uncertain of their position or lacks the necessary skills to execute a task, they are unlikely to wish to take it on. If you give your child a job around the house, ensure that you devote sufficient time to explain how to carry it out and address any concerns your child may have.

To provide suggestions for how to keep it simpler, it may also be a great idea to monitor them a few times. A little coaching from families can help kids deal with challenging homework, but also make sure that your child knows how important it is to speak out in class when they don't comprehend a subject or a home task. Be explicit about what you want from your youngster after schooling as well. Make it plain for your youngster that playing video games comes after finishing their schoolwork. Your kid can be maintained on track and prevented from procrastinating by using a chart or weekly plan.

They can still get away with it because kids are intelligent and can detect deception in their parents from a young age. Don't be shocked if your kid puts off the duty the next time you assign it if you warn to deprive them of TV time in case of not tidying up their bedroom, but then do not comply with the penalty. Follow through after making sure that your child is aware of their obligations, the due date, and the penalties for failing to complete the task. That might encourage your child to take on the responsibilities more carefully and comply when requested.

Procrastination and perfection often coexist because people are frightened of doing something incorrectly or inadequately. Your role is to inspire or prepare your kid for responsibilities if you believe they are evading them just because they lack the self-assurance or knowledge to handle it. Teenagers in their preteen years may be terrified of failing, and many may not always realize that experience is a great educator. Instruct your child that battling through errors is what practice is all about and that parents don't anticipate doing it correctly the first time; if they postpone practicing an instrument out of fear of sounding horrible.

They have to rest: Indeed, kids occasionally put off doing their jobs or their homework since they have more fun activities to engage in, such as being with friends, watching TV, or going to the movies. Make sure that your child has leisure time each day, and try to plan duties at a time when there are fewer distractions. As for schoolwork, some kids require a little rest after school to unwind before actually taking on extra studies. Try to develop a routine that accommodates your kid's requirements, and afterwards, assist your kid in adhering to it. If you believe your kid's calendar is too full, you might want to take out any unimportant events.

2.5 How to Kill Procrastination?

Being in class all day long, especially for a kid with learning difficulties, can be demanding. It may be excessive to ask students to complete more homework at home. Procrastination can be significantly influenced by worry in contrast to annoyance and fatigue. The thought of studying causes an emotional response, which may cause students to postpone their assignments.

Most of us engage in negative mindset characteristics for ourselves, such as "There is no way I can satisfy everyone" or "I am not satisfactory enough." By understanding that children feel anxious and predicated on these feelings, we can teach individuals to replace them with a more favorable thought pattern. *Following Suggestions are worth Considering:*

Recognize the Negative Thoughts

Typically, the same thing is used repeatedly. Gain some insight into your kid's thinking by allowing them to express how he thinks, even if you disagree. Typical thoughts include "I cannot ever do this on my own," "I'm dumb," "If I don't do this correctly, I'll get into problems," and that "People constantly ask a lot of me."

Communication should be put off if your kid is unhappy. Encourage anything he does to help him restore his calm and assure him that everything will be better once he is prepared to avail an opportunity to cool off.

Ask your child to think on his/her positive traits and strengths and fill the following sheets to remove the negativity. Make your kid practice this worksheet often to develop positivity.

Name _____   Date _____

Positive Thoughts

I am
awesome
at........

Assist Your Kid in Feeling Acknowledged

He must know that you comprehend his viewpoint, even if you disagree. Urge him to change his perspective by saying, "I know you're wondering that this is difficult, but let's give it some dedicated tries".

Make a Simple and Stepped Plan

What can he do to make things better? Ask him. If he is stuck in his thoughts, offer alternatives like giving the work a sensible time restriction or approaching the teacher. Suppose your kid is unable to speak up for himself. In that case, you can communicate with the instructor to see if the allocation can be changed (for example, by reducing the amount of time required to complete it, making it simpler, or letting your kid turn in whatever he is capable of doing). You might receive that modification in written form since many children think that their instructors won't even accept an incomplete assignment.

Appreciate Small Achievements

There are several "have to..." expressions that a child may become bored of hearing. Instead of denying it, we should admit that schoolwork is challenging. Think about complementing a schoolwork session with a guilt-free pleasure session. Even if the work is finished in little sections, it is still preferable to achieve something than nothing. He will probably realize that the job is easier than it once appeared, but don't urge extending the duration too promptly or significantly. Increase the work component of the deal gradually while maintaining some fun time as your kid improves his norms.

Limit Your Expectations

It's common to have feelings of insufficiency and success-related anxiety. Your child could be worried that performing well would result in expecting higher from him or giving false high hopes. Rather than setting goals for your child depending on where you'd like them to end up, you have to establish realistic goals.

Give Your Kid Praise

Commend him on effort rather than outcome!

If you understand that procrastination is a coping mechanism for anxiety, you'll be a bit less upset when your kid attempts to postpone or hide having some due work. The benefits of using a successful technique are that your kid won't feel so guilty or difficult, that certain work will get done, and that you can act as a supporting caregiver rather than the assignment enforcer.

Chapter 3: How to Manage Time Effectively?

Kids are generally more energetic and active than most of the adults of today. However, in all the excitement of performing different activities, kids may find it hard to manage their time effectively. It requires them to follow a set routine throughout the day where they designate a specific time to specific activity.

3.1 Getting Out of Bed on Time

For most kids, getting to school early is challenging. Kids require roughly 9 hours of sleep daily for ideal growth and functioning. Nevertheless, studies have revealed that most kids sleep for less than 7 hours per night. The ability to get up early in the morning and leave sleep on days when you don't feel like it is a life skill, notwithstanding kids' natural sleep cycles. Train your kid to do this now to get to school on time.

Get Rid of the Gadgets in The Bedroom

Establish limitations on your child's use of electronics. The effects of excessive television viewing on sleep are numerous. Don't let your kid use a computer or a cell phone in his bedroom at night. Your kid could be tempted to respond if he gets a texting message from a close friend at two in the morning. If he has accessibility to it, he might also be inclined to visit his accounts on social media in the late hours of the night.

Teenagers occasionally choose to watch TV as they sleep. However, watching TV all evening might also make it difficult to sleep well. Decide a time for the TV to be turned off if your kid has one in his bedroom.

Plan your Bedtime

The majority of parents set their standards for sleep during the teen years. More independence is appropriate for kids, but if there are no boundaries for going to bed, kids may stay up even until the early hours of the day. To promote sound sleeping habits, advise on when to go to bed.

Make Weekend Sleep Regulations

Teenagers may be tempted to sleep all day and stay up late on weekends and during school breaks. This may completely disrupt their plans during the academic week. When you get off days, don't sleep all day. Set an appropriate sleep and wake-up timings for yourself even at weekends or holidays.

Avoid Taking Afternoon Naps

When your kid arrives from school, you may want to sleep. However, that can disrupt your nightly sleep, perpetuate your pattern of staying awake late and experiencing fatigue throughout the day. Think of doing exercise, outside activities, and an early sleep if you return home from school feeling exhausted.

3.2 Setting Your Priorities

Even for grownups, teaching kids how to prioritize their activities can be challenging. You may think that you can or must complete everything, but this is never the case. We all understand that certain tasks should always be completed before others. However, the challenge is figuring out what must be done right away and what can wait.

Most parents don't know much about how to effectively educate their kids. Even adults develop their tasks and skills for time management with consistent practice. It is a task that requires consistent and continuous efforts. Multiple project prioritization is still a common problem. Even the people at the top of the management hierarchy in any system have trouble managing their schedules and tasks.

Picture your kid having to choose what to do initially and what not when there are numerous things surrounding him. Both adults and children experience this. You might try to show the kid how to prioritize their duties and do them in the correct sequence as a teacher or parent to make their life easier.

Everything that enables kids to have fun is more important to them than everything else. Although having fun is important, kids should also learn to put other things first, including schoolwork, online learning programs, assisting with modest household tasks, or supporting any younger sisters they may have, etc. Kids should be taught by their parents and instructors how to prioritize things by ranking them from most crucial to least essential or items that can wait till later. They will benefit from it in all of their future endeavors, including their schooling and employment.

We all realize now how crucial time management is for our kids. Do we occasionally concentrate on issues that hinder individuals and cause ongoing worry? We must examine our life carefully and watch for significant pressures. You can start setting priorities for your work by taking the following path:

a. Every Day is a Fresh Start

Take a few minutes each day to make a list of everything you need to or want to accomplish that day. Ask yourself beforehand about your priorities, and afterwards, make yourself understand that how you believe something is essential and, therefore, should come first.

As a parent, you must be aware that what could appear more significant to you could not be to a child. As a result, you must be cautious when outlining the significance of certain points and ensuring that they comprehend your perspective. Setting both long- and short-term goals will help your youngster realize that not all duties can be completed in a given day. The process of learning should be viewed as a chance to acquire new knowledge each day.

b. Record it for them

Make a list of everything that has to be accomplished and jot it down in a book. Sort tasks into three categories: *most essential, next-most significant, and least significant.*

Additionally, you might require your kid to create this checklist each day and assist them in reaching their objectives. Taking notes can be helpful since the youngster can follow a visual guide rather than what has been presented vocally. In this activity, you should also consider your kid's perspectives to determine what matters to them more. Each task's timing, effort, and required skills should be discussed separately with each kid and how they would prefer to proceed. The main goals are to simplify the procedure and let kids express themselves.

c. Important vs Urgent

Everyday life is filled with several significant things. Nevertheless, some must be addressed immediately, whereas others require less immediate attention. What will happen if a given task is completed later? Tell your kid. This will educate the youngster on how to make decisions and will assist him in understanding whatever demands their urgent attention.

They may occasionally select options that are not as urgent, but this is all part of learning. Kids acquire how to prioritize chores and distinguish between urgency and importance through these errors.

Kids can use the following worksheet as an example for prioritizing tasks.

Priortizing Tasks

Priorities urgent, important and less important tasks

Urgent

Important

Less Importnt

d. Guidance

Task management is more complicated than it initially appears. Even adults struggle to complete tasks based on importance. It may take some time for parents and teachers to educate children to prioritize tasks because, to a child, having fun right now may be more important than doing their schoolwork or tidying their bedroom.

This is because they will be confused about what comes first. Therefore, you must intervene and instruct him. One crucial point to remember is that kid's priorities might shift over time, requiring you to stay informed about what's truly going through their heads. Knowing what changed the situation will help you to express yourself in the most effective manner possible. It will increase their likelihood of communicating with you directly about responsibilities and foster a sense of connection.

e. Permit Playtime

It takes time to show your youngster how to prioritize their tasks. Your kid will also have to do that regularly. It should take up most of the day, even if they have to study it. How can you prioritize your to-do list so that you can still find time for yourself later in the day?

Children can take more time than expected to complete a task due to distractions. Although prioritizing work for children is important to help them get the most out of the leisure, parents must also be honest about what can be accomplished. Everybody merits a vacation and a good time. Kids' lives today can get incredibly monotonous. Therefore, it's crucial for them to occasionally get distracted in order to refuel. Let them explore so that they can learn about life's fluidity. These pauses will allow students to fit in time for entertainment and other pursuits as they acquire other valuable skills to advance in their managerial work skills.

Teaching the kids how to schedule their days and control their time is crucial. By getting started earlier, you are building the groundwork for job management and giving them a much more structured day. This supports school achievement and wellness in addition to time efficiency.

3.3 Role of Parents

When you discuss time management, it's not merely about how to add more hours to the day to complete everything done; it's also about making the most of your day. To assist with that, we have put together a list of advice that will demonstrate to your children the value of time management.

Whether they are doing schoolwork or other responsibilities, children are constantly occupied. Due to this, it's critical to instill in them the importance of time management, so they do not even waste their leisure time rushing around attempting to complete everything at once. Children should learn such skills because a happy family is well-organized.

Help Your Children Develop Time Management Skills
Children should be taught time management skills since doing so will benefit individuals in the future as they tackle

bigger and trickier activities. Encourage your children to develop their objectives and divide them into more manageable tasks. They will see that having everything accomplished is possible with some planning and time managerial skills in this manner.

Teach Children Time Management Skills

Even though there are softwares and applications available to assist individuals in organizing their time, if you wish your children to pick up these abilities on their own, you should start by teaching children since toddling years.

Educate your children about a planner that offers sections for daily tasks and lengthier tasks that may necessitate more time. They could gauge the time it takes to complete various tasks without being overburdened by doing them at once.

Managing Children's Time

Giving your children a feeling of the organization while they are still young will help ensure that it is ingrained in their daily lives. Teach your children how to prioritize tasks by listing them in order of importance. By doing so, kids will understand how to divide their time into manageable tasks.

3.4 Learning to Control Impulses

Impulse control can be difficult for many children, especially younger ones, even though it is normal for their developmental phase. Nevertheless, it is a crucial ability that may be developed and enhanced at any time. This is significant since a lack of impulsive behavior causes many behavioral issues. Spontaneous habits tend to normalize, get ingrained, and deteriorate with time without intervention strategy.

When children don't get their way, a restless 5-year-olds may strike or throw fits. In contrast, impulsive 14-year-olds can post offensive stuff on social media or become a victim to even more harmful activities like drinking alcohol without even considering the consequences.

As they get older, you can assist your kid in developing better impulse control. In contrast, research suggests that strengthening such abilities can benefit greatly from therapies to enhance impulse control (as well as other aspects of executive function).

According to studies, ineffective impulse control is associated with bad judgement, the emergence of mental health problems, and poor decision-making. Therefore, the more self-control your child develops, the less probable it is that they would act or do something that may harm others, and the more probable it is that they will have a good mental state.

Impulsive control issues in children with executive functioning personal skills are possible. The methods suggested by the research serve as a manual for teaching impulse control to youngsters' for better classroom teaching, consciousness, and attentiveness. Perhaps you are aware of a youngster who simply cannot control himself in the classroom. They are the ones who talk out, cut off other people's sentences, get up from their seats, and annoy other peers. These behaviors have underlying reasons, which should be considered while treating impulse-related behaviors. Unmet needs, problems with self-control, difficulties articulating oneself, psychological reasons, or other underlying problems can be blamed.

3.5 Getting Rid of Time-Wasting Habits

Our children are more engaged than ever! They have many requirements for their time, including school, schoolwork, socializing, extra-curricular activities, and gadgets. Kids need to control their time well and maintain attention when working on something essential, like schooling and after school studying. You may assist your children in understanding the importance of time by using some of the suggestions and tips in the lines that follow.

Technology
There is no doubt that technology is a part of our daily lives, and this is also true for children. We are connected, educated, and entertained by technologies. However, it's simple for our little folks to develop a technological obsession. Kids are reported spending up to 9 hours per day online, on aggregate, according to some surveys. Although it may also be done on iPad, laptops, computer games, or other gadgets, most people do this on their smartphones. The largest time waster on this list is often technology.

Disorganization
Maintaining impressions is only one aspect of someone being organized. Having a tidy room and home allows children to work more productively but the reverse will occur if chaos

and disorganization gain precedence. Lack of organization makes finding what you need harder, increasing diversions and stress levels. All of that results in a significant amount of time being squandered.

Multitasking

Although it might first appear to be a good idea, handling numerous tasks simultaneously has been shown to waste time and generate results that are of worse value, much like delaying. Even worse, multitasking is prone to frustration and might result in postponement of all of majority of the tasks. Even multitaskers who believe they are adept at it waste time when they should concentrate on one activity at a time.

3.6 Introduce Reward System

Parents may employ a reward system as a method of punishment and behavioral therapy to encourage their children to swap out undesirable actions for happy thoughts. Children are rewarded for good behavior rather than being disciplined for bad behavior. Reinforcement helps children alter their actions and make better decisions. In the end, when a youngster receives support, praise, and incentives for making the right decision, they are more likely to return to such behaviors rather than the negative ones.

It's crucial to consider your child's interests while creating a rewards program. Especially with young children, you shouldn't set expectations for them that aren't a time of life or try to make too many changes in one go. The incentive must be something that your kid wants, that you can use consistently, and that has a reachable objective. Engaging your kid in creating the reward system is the most successful approach to ensure the desired outcomes. Start by asking them whatever they believe makes a good incentive.

It's crucial that the work, the incentive, and the time constraint change with the child's age. A sticker sheet may need to change to one with check boxes or the usage of tokens, play money, or "dollars" they may put toward a larger reward because different reasons probably drive differently-aged children. Kids react better at teenage to more concrete incentives.

When first establishing a reward system, showing school-aged kids a visual display of the activities that earn incentives can be motivating. Offering them a check [or a token] each day can encourage them to work toward their objective, such as allowing them to choose their favorite meal after five days of assisting in cleaning the house. Kids of this age also can manage more complicated benefit packages, so if you choose, you may work on larger objectives or two actions at once. Just ensure that your kid consistently earns prizes. Children in primary school still value regular awards and compliments for their efforts and dedication.

For a school-aged kid, an instance of an incentive may be that they get more time on screen for each afternoon that they finish all of their schoolwork without being asked to.

Possibly Remove Some Marks
The mechanics of the incentive chart are determined by the

parents, as some choose to deduct points for misconduct. If this occurs, make sure your youngster understands the logic behind it.

Add a Time Component

Does your child tend to put things off? Then make sure your reward system has a time-sensitive component! For instance, kids may have to finish their duties before supper or clean their beds by 10 a.m. to accumulate points.

Consult with Your Children

Discuss with your child about possible motivating prizes that are simple to obtain. For instance, if you currently have bookcases full of books, they may well not care about obtaining a new one. However, they might be pining for a group bicycle ride to the newest ice cream shop.

Be Reliable

Objectives are plainly stated on incentive charts, but they only function as much as you persist. Even the smallest star charts necessitate a great deal of work and effort to create. You must have an eye on your children and watch what they do and how they do it.

Chapter 4: Kids' Activities for Time Management Skills

The kids benefit from managing time exercises by enhancing their chances of success in everyday life. It might be challenging to teach young children the skills for time management. Many parents try to instill good time management habits in young kids and it can be made possible with the help of a weekly planner activity given below.

Name _____   Date _____

Weekly Planner
Write your weekly plan to manage your week.

Monday		To do list
Tuesday		
Wednesday		
Thursday		Goal of the week
Friday		
Saturday	Sunday	
Notes		

4.1 Easy to Follow Activities

a. A Puzzle-Making Exercise

This activity aids in teaching your children to avoid wasting time on pointless activities.

Name _____   Date _____

Help the boy to reach the chest below.

b. Filing Dish

Putting stones of various sizes into pots to fill them. It enables your child to understand the value of doing the things that are necessary initially and the less important things later.

c. Activity in the Hourglass

Ask the child to finish any work before one-half of the hourglass empties by creating an hourglass out of a plastic, string, glue, and sand sheet. Your children will benefit from this exercise regarding time management and planning different activities.

d. Worksheet for Assignment

The chore of giving a written assignment on the worksheets is yet another intriguing exercise. Give your kids a job to finish in a certain amount of time. For instance, they might be instructed to draw anything that they find interesting in 5 minutes; the person who finishes it first wins. Your child will understand the significance of time with this game.

Kids Check:

Try the following worksheet to manage the house chores assigned to you. Tick the tasks you did and cross others.

Name _____   Date _____

Daily Check List for House Chores

MORNING

- [ ] Make my bed
- [ ] Get dressed
- [ ] Eat breakfast
- [ ] Brush my teeth
- [ ] Brush my hair
- [ ] Bring lunch
- [ ] Put shoes & socks on

AFTERNOON

- [ ] Wash hands
- [ ] Eat snack
- [ ] Do homework
- [ ] Read for   mins
- [ ] Free play
- [ ] Practice piano
- [ ]

EVENING

- [ ] Set out clothes & shoes
- [ ] Pack backpack
- [ ] Take a shower/bath
- [ ] Put on Pajama
- [ ] Put clothes in hamper
- [ ] Brush teeth
- [ ]

CHORES

- [ ] Set table?
- [ ] Load dishwasher?
- [ ] Wipe dinning table?
- [ ] Pick up toy?
- [ ]
- [ ]
- [ ]

Creating Calendars

Kids can have fun creating a colorful planner to help them organize their time according to the calendar. Ask the child to illustrate the hierarchy of their upcoming tasks using various tables and couples. They become more accountable and reliable as a result of this exercise. Kids can use the following template for this purpose.

Name _____   Date _____

Fill in the following worksheet
to make your customized calander.

Fill year, months, dates and days.
Color differently

The Time-Game

The biggest feature is to educate kids on how to play games that require them to do specified tasks at particular times. Ask the child to give chores a time limit in this exercise, such as 10 minutes for just a toothbrush, 2 hours of play, 15 minutes for a bath. 2 hours for television, etc. Create a list of your daily tasks, give them a specific time, and then stick it on the wall. Highlight the action that your kid completed at the designated time with a checkmark and offer him a prize.

Name _____   Date _____

Write your achievement of the week in
the trophy to give yourself a praise.

The Task Assignment Process

Assign various chores to each family member or form groups in the classroom and give each team member a single job to finish by a certain time. For instance, give your children a small duty like cleaning and warn them that if they fail to do it, dinner will be delayed and everyone in the house will go without food. Through this, the kids will learn that everybody will suffer penalties due to their tardiness. Kids will learn to prioritize finishing the assignment within the time allotted in this way and, as a result, learn time-management skills.

4.2 Quick Tips to Become an Efficient Time Manager

Proper time management advice is crucial for developing organizational skills so kids can organize their lives efficiently right from their childhood. The topmost time management suggestions for children to develop their time management abilities are listed below.

Being Aware

Kids must be aware of what time means to develop their ability to manage time when you instruct your child to complete his assignment in 5 minutes. Can your child get the true meaning of the 5 minutes? Allowing your child to use a clock or timer is fine. They will eventually have the time since they respect the time needed to finish various chores. Bring up the time required to watch their favorite program or get to and from school.

It is really important to teach your child that you cannot do it all at once. Tell your children, for instance, that they cannot attend the family gatherings of two pals at one time and must decide. Making a personal calendar can be a lot of fun for recording significant occurrences like your birth year, the year you moved in, the start of schooling, your first tooth loss, etc. All you need is a roll of paper and a few pictures. Your kids will be able to reach benchmarks throughout time due to this practice.

Recognize a Child's Learning Style

Learn about your kids' learning preferences, so you may modify the environment to accommodate them. The time allotted for that work will be used considerably more effectively, as a result. Kids may favor learning in the company or solo. Despite popular belief, distractions like songs and commotion are not always bad for focus.

The commotion and loudness in the cafeteria, may favor some kids to opt to study there, whereas others choose the calm bookshelves. Some audio-logical researches have indicated that when people listen to songs they appreciate and feel more inclined to study, proving that singing does not hinder learning in some of the children. No specific style of music would help students concentrate greater, but it all relies on their learning preferences. Consequently, it is simpler to develop a working atmosphere when individuals become acquainted. Kids can give themselves a self-evaluation check through the following worksheet.

Name _____   Date _____

Student Self Evaluation

Color the sign which represent your behavior.

I listen when the teacher (or speaker) is talking.	
I follow directions the first time they are given.	
I am polite and respectful to students and adults.	
I ask for help when I don't understand.	
I raise my hand to answer questions in class.	
I take my time and do my best work.	
My work is always neat and I use my best handwriting.	
I finish my work on time.	

Instruct on Time Management

Every kid is born with different perspectives which may or may not match with the people they come in contact with during their entire life. Time management might be more challenging for certain people, but fortunately, it can be studied and acquired like any other academic subject. Practice is an excellent way to improve and learn about this. As with any issue, it's critical to recognize the child's effort and accomplishments while also providing him with advice on how to improve any existing problematic areas. Combined workouts could become enjoyable and easy.

Arranging the Thoughts

Educate your child on how to arrange their thoughts. Inform them that it frequently happens when you have such a lot on your plate that you are unsure of how to start. Jotting down the chores that worry us most will help us organize our ideas and find a solution to this issue.

Teach the kids to arrange their tasks based on the deadline they need to be finished by or according to their objectives to establish the sequence in which they should be done. That becomes simpler to decide how long to spend on any activity each day or throughout the week. These can be placed in a short message to make managing smooth and moving them around the calendar easier.

Create two areas on the cardboard: **(a)** What has to be completed and **(b)** What has already been accomplished. As a result, it will be simple for you to determine when a job is finished and to identify what is still outstanding. When it comes to modest tasks, this practice is very motivating.

Use Pictograms and Symbols to Create Schedules
Pictograms are relatively simple to employ and typically have a great effect on kids. They encourage their independence yet enable them to remember everything. Paste them in the restroom so they can see while washing their hands, brushing their teeth, taking a shower, or combing their hair.

Employ the Instrument for Organization
Pick the item that the child will find most helpful based on each variety's traits. A journal will likely be the best option if a large amount of data must be entered daily to visualize a whole week. A calendar might be more useful to aid in time management if the aim is to mark the highlights of every day. Depending on the work, decide which time management solution to use.

Self-Control
Being told to do something is rarely enjoyable, and accepting responsibility can sometimes be challenging. Therefore, they must be fundamental. We occasionally have to accept the repercussions of our acts to gain insight from our errors. While it may not always be feasible, if it is, just let it socialize in the experience. For others, it may have considerably more appeal. They will develop their sense of accountability in this way. Parents are crucial role models whenever it comes to accountability. The proverb "the apple rarely falls away from the tree" is one that children can learn much more by imitating.

Name _____   Date _____

Triggers and Coping Skills

Write your top ten triggers. In the next block,
write starategy you will prefer to control triggers.

Name _____   Date _____

All My Feelings

Share the times when you feel..........

Happy _____

_____

Angry _____

_____

Disappointed _____

_____

Nervous _____

_____

Embrrassed _____

_____

Confused _____

_____

Sad _____

_____

Conclusion

We all desire to have more hours in the day, but since there are only 24 in a day, it's imperative to utilize them as efficiently as possible. You can utilize your time more effectively if you take the chance to plan, either often or perhaps even at the start of the week. As a result, you'll know whether you are on track to accomplish your goals and any actions that you need to undertake to keep from falling ahead.

There are some benefits to multitasking, but if you use it too frequently, you'll find you're doing a lot while accomplishing very little. You will be more effective during the day if you focus on one task at a time, even for a brief period.

It's quite challenging to be using your time effectively if you don't know what you should do with it. Students should set both long- and short-term goals. It's far too easy to get distracted. Look for anything that keeps you from your work or studies. Whatever else is wasting your time, make it a point not to engage in that behavior throughout your dedicated study time. Instead, use other activities as inspiration to stay motivated and accomplish the goals you set for yourself.

We've all wanted to handle everything on our own but this might easily result in tiredness. You can spend more time on more important activities by outsourcing less important work responsibilities or household chores.